The "POWER" of a strong enough reason

Understanding the "<u>MASTER KEY</u>" that activates " <u>Action Taking Ability</u>", to achieve success in life you were destined for!

By
Michael A. Williams
founder, Positive State U!

Positive State, Positive State U & Positive State University. Copyright 2016.
All rights reserved

CONTENTS

1. Positive Greetings Powerful 3
2. Instructions! Your Greatest Friend 3
3. Nothing Just Happens 9
4. Motivation 10
5. Limitations 11
6. The Power of Decision 13
7. The Two Spiritual Governing Systems 15
8. Strong Reason Activates Bounce Back Ability ..21
9. A Strong Reason To Hope.............................25
10. The Winning Mindset Of Strong Reason..........28
11. By reason of a Dream 38
12. Strong Reason Awakens Unique Gifts 41
13. Strong Reason Ignites Passion.......................45
14. Strong Reason inspires " Go Get ".....................48
15. Success's little Secret 50
16. Strong Reason Empowers Imagination 52
17. The Power of An Image Maker 54
18. Restores pursuit of destined purpose.......56
19. Finding Your Reason 61
20. Understanding Your Destined Purpose 64
21. Give God Something To Work With 67
22. Conclusion 71

Positive greetings "Powerful"!

I call you powerful because dwelling on the inside of you is a treasure of wealth, simply waiting to be discovered. You have been given capability to manifest inner wealth into physical reality, through accomplishment of purposeful dreams and visions. Utilizing your capability to bring your dreams and visions forth into the earth, is something you were destined for.

This capability is what I call, *"goal achieving ability"!* Goal achieving ability enables you to bring anything that you can possibly imagine, into reality! Knowing this is extremely dynamic! Understanding how to operate it purposefully, is "POWERFUL"! Goal achieving ability enables you to take action and achieve any goal that you desire.

However, before you can Take action to achieve a goal, you must first have a desired goal that you want to achieve. Secondly, you must have "How To" instructions to follow in order to bring your goals into reality.

Instructions! Your Greatest Friend

Instructions is the greatest friend you will have, when it comes to achieving your goals.

They are the blue print to follow to birth your vision into reality.

Instructions are always available at the beginning of things. They are often introduced during new beginning moments in your life, such as, at the start of a new job, at the beginning of a school semester, or at the start of a new building project, it does'nt matter. Wherever there are new beginnings, instructions will always come forth, to show you the desired path designed to get you to your destination.

When using a product that was created by another, it often comes with operating instructions. These Instructions are made available by the product creator, to guide the product user on how to get the best possible experience, their product is capable of delivering.

For every creation within the earth, there is a purpose. Within each purpose you will find "How To" Instructions on what that creation is designed to achieve.

The moment you decide to follow "How To" instructions concerning achievement of a thing, your chances greatly increase towards purposely bringing the goal you seek into reality!

It all starts with a mental decision!

You can change the course of your life with one mental decision!
However, making a mental decision begins with your desire!

You will not take action to achieve any goals in your life, until your desire becomes sparked to do so. I call this form of desire, *"Want To"*! "Want To" is that level of desire where reaching your goal has simply become a must for you. This means you have reached the place of having no other option! Achieving your goal has now become something that you must do!

Before you can achieve any goal or dream in your life, you must decide to turn on your *"Want To"*. The moment you turn your "Want To" on, you begin the process of goal achievement! This is because the moment your "Want To" is turned on, Action Taking ability" has become activated!

Taking action is the secret ingredient to achieving goals. As a result, the moment your goals are achieved, the manifestation of your change appears! How do you turn your *"Want To"* on? Your **"Want To"** is turned on the moment you find a strong enough reason to do something.

The moment you find a strong enough reason to do something, you will do whatever is necessary to bring forth your desired goal.

However, only you possess the capability to turn your "Want To" on! No one else can turn it on for you. It does not matter how much someone else desires to see you achieve your goal.

However, when your reason to achieve something becomes strong enough, it will activate your action taking ability, designed to bring your desired goals into manifestation.

Only a strong enough reason, can motivate you to do what you must, in order to obtain your prize.

It is a strong enough reason that gives a winner who is losing a race, inspiration to bounce back and win it in the end. It does not matter what arena the race may happen to be in.

However, although you may have the "How To" information on what to do to achieve your goals and dreams, only a strong enough reason, will inspire you to *take* the necessary action in order to bring them into reality!

When your reason for doing something is strong enough, it activates inner ability within you to do what's necessary to bring forth results you've purposed!

Dr. Martin Luther King Jr, a Phenomenal and Powerful sent visionary, found a strong enough reason to stand against injustice.

Through strong belief in his vision, Martin activated dynamic empowerment, that set in motion change of the civil rights laws in America for African Americans.

Martin's dream to see human equality in America was very Powerful. Through it others were empowered to stand non-violently against a governing system, that only had human equality written as law, but they never supported it.

However, it was the power of Martin's dream that changed the system of an entire nation!

Martin's vision also inspired him to imagine the U.S. as a country, one day having an African American president.

During one of his speech's, Martin spoke life to this vision, confessing it into the atmosphere! It was a vision Martin was given, during a time when African Americans had not been able to exercise their voting rights.

Although he didn't get to see it's physical manifestation, the power of Martin's dream granted his children the opportunity to witness its reality, during their lifetime.

A strong enough reason activates empowerment within you to change or rearrange situations, in order to bring goals you were destined for into reality.

Within this empowering book, you will discover the empowerment of having a strong enough reason, along with the achievements obtained by others, as a result of them having one.

You will also discover how to locate the strong enough reason designed to activate your action taking ability, to bring the visions and dreams you were destined for, into reality.

Nothing Just Happens

Nothing in life just happens! There is a reason behind every action that you take in life!

Reason is the fuel that activates your capability, to rise up to every level of success you were destined for. This transition occurs by you first finding, then taking ownership of your own reason for walking in your appointed destiny!

Michael Jordan, one of the greatest to ever play the game of basketball, was compelled by a strong enough reason to beat his brother in a game of basketball. The results? Through determination and persistent practice habits, Michael uncovered the empowering ability he had dwelling within himself! Utilizing this ability, Michael finally developed his basketball skills to the level needed, to beat his brother! Michael's development caused his skills to promote him to such a level of basketball greatness, that they now have become the standard by which NBA excellence is measured.

Michael found a reason that was strong enough to motivate him to become his best, and he took pursuing action and embraced it. The results? It brought Michael to the place of discovering empowerment to reach his goals. Which he found was always available to assist him the moment his "**Want To**" had become turned on.

Having a Strong enough reason, is the master key to unlocking your "Action Taking ability", that your purposed goals may come into physical manifestation. This is because a strong enough reason gives you motive! Motive activates your drive to take action.

A strong enough reason activates that motivating drive you need to press in, when you're losing at something, to release inner ability to bounce back at the end for the win. A strong enough reason increases within you action taking drive, which I call "motivation", to do what must be done in order to obtain the goal that you seek.

George Forman, former heavyweight boxing champ, found a reason strong enough to motivate him to greatly persist, and bounce back from a twenty year absence away from the world of boxing, to regain the heavy weight title for a second time!

Motivation

Motivation is very powerful! The moment you become motivated to do something, inner strength activates driving force to move and take action.

Investigators, when beginning there pursuit into solving a case, start their search looking for a motive. Because they understand that a strong enough motive is what activates the drive within someone, to commit or to do a specific thing.

Limitations

A strong enough reason does not yield to limitations!
What are limitations! limitations are simply overcomable boundaries we mentally place on ourselves, through negative thought intake. These limitations subconsciously form into part of our belief system over a period of time.

The moment you have found a strong enough reason to achieve your goal, you activate an inner ability that's powerful enough to move all limitations out of your way.

When it came to limitations, Thomas Edison was up against one of his greatest challenges of his life. For he was pursuing achievement of a goal that had no available blue print or " How To" instructions to follow, for bringing it into reality. This is because during that time, light through electricity had not yet been discovered. The only thing Edison had to work with was his determination, persistance and strong belief that his vision was possible to achieve!

This reason was strong enough for Edison to endure nine hundred and ninety nine missed attempts, before finally bringing forth electric light. Thomas Edison discovered how electrical power was harnessed, then developed it to bring light into the world. Today, electrical light has become a natural resource that's unimaginable to live without.

When it comes to achieving destined vision, It doesn't matter the type of odds that are stacked up against you. It doesn't even matter about negativity you may have been told, concerning not having what it takes to succeed at anything!

The moment you find a strong enough reason to achieve the goal you want, then decide to pursue it, this activates your action taking ability to bring your desired goal into Reality.

The Power of Decision

It all starts with a decision. It starts with you first making a decision to pursue your vision or dream!
Achievement of your dreams and visions can only be possible after you make a decision to take action! When your reason to take action becomes strong enough, you will take whatever action thats necessary to bring forth the goal that you desire.

However, the result producing process can only begin, the moment you make a real decision to see your goals come into reality.

Great achievements are manifested in life, as a result of someone making a real decision to go after them.

What do I mean by making a real decision to achieve your goals?
Making a real decision simply means you have really decided to do whatever it will take, in order to obtain the goal that you really want!

However, making a real decision to achieve your desired goal is one of the hardest things you will ever do. Why? Because the moment you make a real decision to achieve your desired goal, you eliminate every other option as a possibility.

The moment you eliminate every other goal achieving option as a possibility,

your real decision has now become a must achieve option for you.

Being placed in a "must achieve" goal situation, simply means that you now have no place else to go, but forward. Whenever you are placed in this situation, it positions you to give focused attention on your specific goal! This produces needed clarity, to bring to light your plan of action.

The Two Spiritual Governing Systems!

The intentions of this book is to highlight the power you activate, the moment you discover a strong enough reason to pursue achievement of your destined vision or dream in life. The challenge sometimes is finding a reason that's strong enough to inspire your pursuit, towards that specific goal!

Therefore, before setting out to achieve something, having a clear understanding of the fields you are allowed to operate from, are very important.

Finding a strong enough reason simply means, finding a purposeful meaning to go after something that you want or desire to achieve. In other words, it means you have found something that you want, which you are determined to go after because you have discovered a fulfilling purpose for achieving it.

When it comes to obtaining success in life, you will only pursue achievement of it, when you have found a fulfilling reason for doing so.

However, it is for this reason along that you were created.

You were created to live a life of heaven upon the earth!

You were designed in the image of your heavenly father, to fulfill His desire for you to be fruitful and multiply in the earth! You see, the father's desire for you from the beginning, has been to rule and dominate in the earth, while replenishing every part of it!

This has always been God's original thought for you from the foundation of the world!

Look at what the book of Genesis reveals to us!

And God blessed them, and God said unto them, Be fruitful, and multiply, and replenish the earth, and subdue it: and have dominion over the fish of the sea, and over the fowl of the air, and over every living thing that moves upon the earth. **(Genesis 1:28)**

However, the moment Adam and Eve sinned in the garden of Eden, they gave up man's empowerment, authority and ownership of the earth, into the hands of their new master, Satan.

Look at what the book of Romans tells us!

Know ye not, that to whom ye yield yourselves servants to obey, his servants ye are to whom ye obey; whether of sin unto death, or of obedience unto righteousness?
(Romans 6:16)

Before Adam and Eve's disobedience in the garden, they were only serving the Lord their father, God of heaven and earth. They were operating within earth, under the law that governs the system of the Kingdom of heaven.

This is the law of faith, which says, whatever the Word of Father God tells you to do, that is what you do! Why? Because only within his word can you find and fulfill, your destined purpose upon the earth!

However, the disobedient actions of Adam and Eve caused them to yield in servanthood to another invisible force. It was through there act, that the operating law of another governing system was introduced. It was the law of fear, which they both became servants to.

Look at what the book of Genesis reveals to us!

And the lord God called unto Adam, and said unto him, Where art thou? And he said, I heard thy voice in the garden, and I was afraid, because I was naked; and I hid myself.
(Genesis 3:9-10)

As a result of heeding to the voice of Satan, Adam & Eve began operating upon the earth under the influence of the spirit of fear.

The spirit of fear is what tainted their view of the perception that God thought about them.

So, what am I saying? I am saying that as a result of Adam and Eves actions in the garden, birth was given to another spiritual governing system.

Therefore, there are now two spiritual governing systems that are in operation upon the earth!

There is the Kingdom of God's system of operation, that is governed by the law of faith!

Then, there is the system of this world, which is governed by Satan, under the influence of the spirit of fear!

However, now through Christ you have been given the opportunity again, to fulfill the purpose God has destined for your life.

What is that purpose? It is for you to be fruitful and multiply within every area of life, while being replenishing all the earth!

This was the purpose of why Jesus came to the earth, to restore you back into your rightful place, through acceptance of what He did for you upon Calvary!

Now, as a born again believer, you have become restored back into the family of God, through Christ by adoption as Abraham's seed!

What does all this have to do with you living successfully now, within your everyday practical life?
This means that now you have a legal right to partake of all the treasures of the whole world!
This is legally yours due to your share of the inheritance that God promised you, as the seed of Abraham.

Look at what the book of Romans reveals unto us!
For the promise, that he should be the heir of the world, was not to Abraham, or to his seed, through the law, but through the righteousness of faith. **(Romans 4:13)**

In other words, what I am saying is that As a child of the Most High God, you have an inheritance that the Lord Jesus has made available for you! Not only that, but God also has a fail proof blueprint for success already laid out for you, to live a life in heavenly paradise while fulfilling Kingdom purpose upon the earth.

God's desire is for you to live an abundantly successful life.
This is the strongest and most fulfilling reason you can have for taking action to make success a reality within your life.

God created you to live in the heavenly paradise of Eden, while dwelling successfully upon the earth!

Strong Reason Activates Bounce Back Ability

The moment you were born again, you were redesigned with winning ability on the inside of you called, dominion!
Dominion is dynamic inner ability that empowers you to achieve the domination of win, in your purposed place of destiny!

When operating in your purposed place you do not compete with others, you only complete your destined assignment. Why? Because only you have been assigned your specific purpose. The purpose you were created to fulfill, holds the place of destiny that was designed personally for you!

When in your destined place of purpose, you will always dominate no matter what situation you encounter. Why? Because from your purposed place, you can always activate your supernatural fight game.

What is your supernatural fight game?
It is your empowering inner ability to execute your faith through Kingdom principles, in all arena's of life! When operating from this space, you are enabled to protect your royal inheritance through domination, while maintaining your eternal position of victory!

The Positive State motivational poster below,
(Motivational posters are tools of inspiration made available from the Positive State U platform, through social media, to promote personal development)
Attempts to highlight that dominating fight game ability, that's dwelling inside of you!

Positive State, Positive State U & Positive State University. Copyright 2016. All rights reserved

In 1968, George Forman came out of nowhere and won the heavy weight boxing Olympic gold medal. Five years later in 1973, he knocked down Joe Frazier 6 times for the heavy weight championship of the world!

After losing his crown a year later to Muhammad Ali, along with a non successful comeback attempt, George felt compelled to retire from the ring in 1977.
10 years later at age 38, George returned to the ring after experiencing destined awakening, with a new found sense of purpose, focus & determination.

After many months of extremely dedicated physical training, George rose to become the oldest heavy weight champion in boxing history! At age 45, he won the title for a second time. George found a strong enough reason for winning again, and bounced back after two decades of being absent, to become a two time world boxing champion.

When operating from your place of purpose, the moment you act on a strong enough reason to win again, access is granted to dominion ability, which activates empowerment for bringing the destiny you were purposed for, into reality.

The Positive State motivational poster below,
(Motivational posters are tools of inspiration made available
from the Positive State U platform, through social media, to
promote personal development)
Attempts to highlight the dynamic capabilities of that
treasure of wealth
that's dwelling inside of you!

Positive State, Positive State U & Positive State University. Copyright 2016.
All rights reserved

A Strong Reason To Hope

Three siblings, found a strong enough reason to unite there voices together in song, after their mother Felicia Cole encountered a near fatal accident. Mom's accident was the result of a head on car collision she was involved in.

Michael, Avery and Nadia, felt compelled to begin singing at their mothers hospital bedside, after this near fatal accident sent her into a coma.

After several months, her condition showed them little to no sign of recovery. These signs, which often shows hopelessness in others, only sparked strong belief within these faith filled siblings, that they would soon see their mother rise again.

It was this belief that gave them inspiration to begin singing at her bedside! From believing hearts filled with passion and faith, they begin to lift their voices with praise unto their God. Before long, their harmonious voices began to give birth to a sound that was GLORIOUS. As a result, the ministry of "***VOICES OF GLORY***" was born.

They soon felt compelled to sing songs of life within the hearts of others, who were also bed ridden in the same hospital.

Quickly, their gifts begin to make room for them, as requests were now being made by other hospitals and churches everywhere.

In 2009, voices of glory auditioned for America's Got talent and landed top five, as contestants.

The result? Three singing siblings became overnight international sensations! They were now heavily in demand the world over! What first began as very small requests, had now risen to include appearances at major venues such as, Madison Square Garden and the annual GMA'S Dove awards.

When your reason to succeed at something becomes strong enough, the sky is the limit as to how far you can go.

What started from a strong desire to see their mother come out of a coma, resulted in the birth of these glorious voices from Branson Missouri. They now travel the world over, uplifting millions with triumphant songs of victory.

Their mother? Well she miraculously recovered!

The Positive State motivational poster below,
(Motivational posters are tools of inspiration made available from the Positive State U platform, through social media, to promote personal development)
Attempts to inspire your desire to envision your desired goal!

Positive State, Positive State U & Positive State University. Copyright 2016. All rights reserved

The Winning Mindset Of Strong Reason

Through relationship in Christ, your success has already been inherited! However, to obtained it, takes operating from a winning mindset!

A winning mindset is a mind that has been set on following the development principles of an already proven result getting plan.

This means, when you have purposed to do something, your mind has already been made up and focused on bringing your goal into reality.

When your mind is already made up, it means you have set or programed it to think a particular way.

This planned out thought process is mental strategy that you set in place purposely by design, to bring whatever goal you are pursuing into reality.

Consistent winning is the result of having your mind set on principles which you are following, from an already proven winning strategy. Jesus has become our champion. He has become everlasting winner, achieving the title of champion of "Success In Life"! Through him, you no longer have to toil in order to achieve success if life, you simply have to accept it.

Through faith in him, you have now become victorious, and empowered to overcome any obstacle you will ever encounter within any arena of life.

Look at what the book of first John tells us.

For whatsoever is born of God overcomes the world: and this is the victory that overcomes the world, even our faith. ***(1 John 5:4)***

You were designed to win! However it is you that have to set your mind to follow the Success principles God has already laid in place, for obtaining winning results.

Look at what the book of Deuteronomy reveals to us.

I have set before you life and death, blessing and cursing: therefore choose life, that both thou and thy seed may live:
(Deuteronomy 30:19)

God has already set before you the winning strategies for obtaining success in life. Therefore he is telling you to choose them.

These proven principles obtains God's strategies for achieving success in life. These principles are those which governs His Kingdom.

At the end of the day when all the smoke clears, winning in the earth is all about getting results.

The moment you decide to line your mind up with Kingdom principles, It is the moment you position yourself for achievement of winning success!

This takes operating at the highest level of confidence. A feat you are totally equipped to achieve. This means all you have to do is place your confidence in God!
When you operate with confidence placed in God, you get results.

Here's what King David declared about the result getting ability of Kingdom principles:

I have been young, and now am old; yet have I not seen the righteous forsaken, nor his seed begging bread. **(Psalms 37:250)**

King David experienced the wonderful privilege of seeing the proven winning results of Kingdom principles, time and time again. Which begin back in the days of his youth.

Within every situation David encountered, he was always motivated by a strong enough reason to see God's power show up on his behalf.

When the power of God showed up for David to destroy the lion, this gave him a strong enough reason to believe He would see the power show up to deliver him from the bear, which it did. The power also showed up for David to defeat Goliath, giant of the philistine army.

After seeing God's power show up within all of his encounters, King David became expectant when it came to believing for God's power to show up in his life!

As a result, David developed to a place of believing he would see God's goodness show up within all the land.

Look at what the book of Psalms reveals to us!

I had fainted, unless I had believed to see the goodness of the Lord in the land of the living.
(Psalms 27:13)

Placing your confidence in what God has said, will develop within you a habit of expecting to see consistent wins in your life! This is because you will come to discover that Kingdom principles does not have the option to fail!

Look at what the book of Isaiah reveals to us:

So shall my word be that goes forth out of my mouth: it shall not return unto me void, but it shall accomplish that which I please, and it shall prosper in the thing whereto I sent it. (Isaiah 55:11).

The wisdom of God is the Kingdom's principles for winning!
Therefore, whenever you set your mind to follow God's kingdom principles, you position yourself for consistent winning. Because God's Word will only produce accomplishment. This is a result of you only praying God's word back to him. Here, results takes place. Results produces confidence in God.

Look at what the book of first John reveals to us!

And this is the confidence that we have in him, that, if we ask any thing according to his will, he heareth us:

And if we know that he hear us, whatsoever we ask, we know that we have the petitions that we desired of him. (1 John 5:14,15)

The Positive State motivational poster below,
*(Motivational posters are tools of inspiration made available
from the Positive State U platform, through social media, to
promote personal development)*
**Attempts to inspire Mindset development towards your
desired goal!**

Positive State, Positive State U & Positive State University. Copyright 2016.
All rights reserved.

As a child of God, always remember, you have
been empowered with the victorious of mind of
Christ!

Look at what the book of first Corinthians reveals
to us!

*For who hath known the mind of the Lord, that he may instruct him? but we have the mind of Christ. **(1 Corinthians 2:16)***

Jesus walked on the earth with the mindset of one having Higher authority!

Look at what the book of Matthew reveals to us!

*And when he was come into the temple, the chief priests and the elders of the people came unto him as he was teaching, and said, By what authority does thou these things? and who gave thee this authority? **(Matthew 21:24)***

This is because Jesus had a clear understanding concerning his identity!
He knew he was the son of the most high God!
Jesus walked upon the earth as a man on destined assignment!

Jesus was convinced of two things!
One: He was convinced that whatever he needed to fulfill his destined assignment, was already granted by his father.

Two: Jesus walked with confidence knowing that whatever the word of God said, would surely come to pass!

Lets Look at what the book of Isaiah reveals to us !

*So shall my word be that goeth forth out of my mouth: it shall not return unto me void, but it shall accomplish that which I please, and it shall prosper in the thing whereto I sent it. **(Isaiah 55:11)***

Because of Jesus's understanding of this, He walked through earth towards destiny in a Positive attitude of great Joy!

Look at what the book of Hebrews reveals to us!

*Looking unto Jesus the author and finisher of our faith; who for the joy that was set before him endured the cross, despising the shame, and is set down at the right hand of the throne of God. **(Hebrews 12:1)***

When you operate with a mind that is fully confident in God and his word, it places your attitude in a Joyfully positive state!

When Joshua was given the assignment to take the children of Israel into their land of promise, God commanded him to operate from a positive mental state.

God knew Joshua would be dealing with people whose attitudes often changed, causing them to always be feeling some kind of way.

Moses was graced to witness God's mighty deliverance power many times, like when he watched God part the red sea for Israel to reach the other side. However, because he allowed Israel's disobedience to have a negative effect on his attitude, he angrily smote a rock and wasn't allowed to enter into the promise land.

As a result, the assignment of taking them in was given to Joshua! God gave Joshua a two option attitude command, which was only to be strong and very courageous. That his mission may be fulfilled and his assignment carried out.

Look at what the book of Joshua reveals to us.

Have not I commanded thee? Be strong and of a good courage; be not afraid, neither be thou dismayed: for the Lord thy God is with thee whithersoever thou goes.
(Joshua 1:9)

The winning attitude mindset always will say, "one of these attempts at achievement are going to work"!

While the mindset that fails says, "I will try this one more time, if it doesn't work, I quit"!

Now, let me ask you a question?

If it took Thomas Edison nine hundred and nine missed attempts, before discovering Electricity, which one of these attitude mindsets do you think he operated from?

" I will try one more time, if it doesn't work, I quit "?
Or?
" One of these attempts are going to work "?
Of course! It was, "One of these attempts are going to work"!

When operating from a mindset that has placed it's trust in God and his word, there is no such thing as failure, with each missed attempt you simply know what not to do next time!

Now you have been given the authority to operate in the earth, utilizing the same mindset christ operated from.

Look at what the book of Philippians reveals to us.

*Let this mind be in you, which was also in Christ Jesus: **(Philippians 2:5)***

By Reason Of A Dream

Joseph was an Israelite who had eleven brothers! Because of the strong belief he had in his God given dream, Joseph encountered a season of imprisoned slavery during his young adult life.

This resulted simply from Joseph's passion to share his dream with close family. However, during Joseph's season of imprisonment he walked in total success towards fulfillment of his dream.
This is due to the achieving power of God being heavily revealed within every arena of Joseph's life.

For Joseph was a man who chose to believe in God, when it came to the future outcome of his life!
At no time did Joseph ever choose to waiver! As a result, everything that Joseph set out to achieve became a reality, even while he was yet a imprisoner!

In the book of Genesis, during every phase of Joseph's journey, he was described as a successful and prosperous man! Why? Because the Lord God was in partnership with him!

Look at what the amplified version of Genesis reveals to us!

The Lord was with Joseph, and he [even though a slave] became a successful and prosperous man; **(Genesis 39:2 Amplified)**

Within the Kingdom, you do not become successful as a result of any performance you have achieved! You are successful because of your relationship with God! This means your success in the Kingdom is a result of your identity, and not because of what you achieve.

Just as Joseph recognized, when you operate from your place of destined purpose, you will increase and prosper in everything that you do. It does not matter where you happen to find yourself.

Not only that, but the blessings that will manifest as a result of who you are, will have a noticeable impact on those all around you.

Look what the book of Genesis reveals to us!

And his master saw that the Lord was with him, and that the Lord made all that he did to prosper in his hand. **(Genesis 39:3)**

The Positive State motivational poster below,
(Motivational posters are tools of inspiration made available
from the Positive State U platform, through social media to
promote personal development)
Attempts to inspire pursuit towards your destined visions
and dreams!

Positive State, Positive State U & Positive State University. Copyright 2016.
All rights reserved

Strong reason awakens Unique Gifts

You have been given a unique gift, which makes you different from everyone else. You have been equipped with your gift to carry out and fulfill destined purpose.
You have been uniquely designed, to deliver empowerment towards bettering the lives of an assigned audience.

Your gift is the personalized key you were given to unlock the wealth treasure you have dwelling deep within you.

It was the awakening of Joseph's unique gift to interpret dreams, that unlocked the phenomenal wealth treasure that was awaiting him!

Look at what the book of Genesis reveals to us!

And there was there with us a young man, an Hebrew, servant to the captain of the guard; and we told him, and he interpreted to us our dreams; to each man according to his dream he did interpret. **(Genesis 41:12)**

Belief that he would see his dream becoming reality, served as his strong enough reason to endure a season of slavery, until his gift made room for him to rise and become second in command of the entire country.

As Joseph also discovered, your inner gift empowers you to manifest the wealth you were destined for. The moment you decide to use your gifts to speak wisdom into hearts you were assigned to, you will be promoted into high places within the earth and marketplace.

Look what the book of proverbs reveals to us!

Doth not wisdom cry? and understanding put forth her voice? She standeth in the top of high places, by the way in the places of the paths.
(proverbs 8:1-2)

The moment your gift has been taken to the marketplace it becomes available for God to use, to empower the lives of the specific audience you were destined to serve.

Oftentimes, voices operating under influence from this world's system will try to convince you, that there is no room for your gift within the market place.

When in truth, the earth is waiting for the release of that greatness which dwells inside of you.

Look at what the book of Romans reveals to us!

For the earnest expectation of the creature waiteth for the manifestation of the sons of God. **(Romans 8:19)**

Your presence upon the earth, is evidence your life has great significance! There is strong need for the unique gift that God has placed within you.

King Solomon said, *"A man's gift makes room for him, and bringeth him before great men"!* ***(proverbs 18:16)***

It is your gift that carries the solution to a problem, someone else urgently needs to have resolved in their life.

There will always be strong demand for your gift when you give it to God.

God has need of your gift to assist with advancement of his Kingdom!

Helping others become better is the very essence of what true success is all about.

Success is becoming the very best person you can possibly be, in all areas of life.

However, to become the very best person that you can possibly be,
comes by helping someone else become the very best person that they can be.

The Positive State motivational poster below,
(Motivational posters are tools of inspiration made available from the Positive State U platform, through social media, to promote personal development)

Attempts to highlight the power of your uniqueness!

Positive State, Positive State U & Positive State University. Copyright 2016.
All rights reserved.

Strong reason ignites Passion

Through Joseph's phenomenal passion, we learned that your gift will make room for you in the marketplace! However, the inspiration behind your gift will cause it to burn like a fire, that others may experience it's impact.

This inspiring fire is what I call, passion! Passion is a fire that will cause your gift to spread without limits.

While growing up in chicago, we often witnessed houses within our neighborhood catch on fire. Each time they did no matter day or night, people within our community would always come out to see that house fire burn.

The inspiring passion you display when using your gift, activates desire within the hearts of others to want to experience it.

Your passion is the secret ingredient that places your gift in much demand.

Passion is an inner empowerment which activates, the moment you engage in doing something you truly enjoy and love to do.

It is something you would find yourself doing whether you get paid for doing it or not.

Utilization of your gift is the vehicle which releases your inner greatness into the world.

The moment you begin using your gift, your passion begins to develop, the more your passion develops, the more room will be made for you.

Great joy is associated with making your gift available within the world.

This great joy begins the moment your gift is discovered and developed! All of which occurs the moment you have found a strong enough reason for delivering your gift into the world.

Passion often manifests whenever you are exercising your gift.

As the world begins to experience the dynamic impact of your unique gift, your passion will connect them to the empowerment it carries. The moment you give spark to your gift, it will begin burning like fire, then people will come from places far away, just to see your inspiring fire burn.

The Positive State motivational poster below,
(Motivational posters are tools of inspiration made available
from the Positive State U platform, through social media, to
promote personal development)
Attempts to inspire your pursuit towards igniting of
passion!

Positive State, Positive State U & Positive State University. Copyright 2016.
All rights reserved.

Strong reason inspires " Go Get "!

Everything that you need to manifest your inner greatness, has been made available to you. A strong enough reason inspires the determined to set their mind towards seeing something in God, and then go get it!

Great accomplishers, of whom some we've highlighted within this book, have left marks of achievement that has greatly empowered the lives of many. I call them, go getters!

Go getters operate in life from a position of strong reason to achieve. Once they have found a reason that's strong enough do something, they visualize their goal, develop a plan to obtain it, then they go get it! They operate from a mindset of planned purpose.

Go getters plant seeds that cause goal achievement manifestation. Go getters are simply those who're motivated by purpose they believe they've been destined for.
Go getter's dare to believe that obtaining their goals are not only a possibility, but it is a **must**".

As a result, there determination does not comprehend quitting or giving up, only pursuit, until the goal they seek has been manifested!

Go getters operate from that winning mindset which only expects to see goal accomplishment.

They are those who simply Go and get what they strongly believe is rightfully there's.

Success's little Secret

To become the best person you can possibly be, comes by helping someone else become the best they can be.

This statement embodies the true essence of success!

It is connected to helping better the life of another!

You show me the owner of a successful restaurant chain, and I will show you someone who rose to the challenge of bringing great food service to there customers.

You show me the owner of a successful car dealership, and I will show you someone who rose to the challenge of bringing great vehicle service to their customers.

A great leader within any arena, is simply someone who has become great at serving others. Therefore, for this very reason, that phenomenal gift you have dwelling within you, was given.

To rise to the challenge of serving others, that they may strive towards becoming their very best in life.

You have been blessed with your gift, simply to be a blessing in the life of another!

Strong reason empowers Imagination!

Within you, dwells many great empowering tools. Your phenomenal imagination is one of these great empowerments.

Imagination is an essential tool which causes you to birth your goals and dreams into the world. Through your imagination, you get to bring to life any idea you can simply imagine.

Imagination gives you the opportunity to take mental pictures of your ideas, before they have been introduced to the physical eye.

Imagination is the holding tank which stores your inner ideas! Your ideas are also recognized as possibilities. I call these possibilities, potential.

Within your potential dwells unlimited possibility! The moment you begin to visualize a possibility, this idea enters your imagination and becomes available for being birthed.

Your potential is filled with possibilities that are just waiting on you to connect them with vision, which gives them purpose.

God has a dynamic plan designed for everything he has given you, including your imagination. ***(Jerimiah 29:11 Amplified)***

The moment your vision has been connected to purpose, that's when you've found your strong enough reason for brining your vision out of your imagination and into reality.

The Positive State motivational poster below,
(Motivational posters are tools of inspiration made available from the Positive State U platform, through social media, to promote personal development)
Attempts to inspire utilization of your Imagination

Positive State, Positive State U & Positive State University. Copyright 2016. All rights reserved.

The Power of An Image Maker

Through imagination, life was given to a wonderful amusement world which dwelt within the extraordinary potential of Walt Disney!

One of the greatest visionaries of our time, Walt Disney made the world become believers in the animated world he had, living deep within his potential.

Walt's phenomenal imagination gave physical visualization to wealth treasures of animated greatness, that continues to positively impact the lives of others, years after his death.

Here was a visionary so driven by imagination, that at age seven, he began selling sketches of his designed images to his neighbors.

Walt found unusual places to give visual life to his visions. Once, he convinced his sister to help him design one of his animations on the side of their house, using a can of tar.

Walt's strong passion for animation once compelled him to completely design his car with animated characters!

Oh, did I forget to mention it was a company car for the American red cross, which he was hired to drive while chauffeuring their officials around during the time of war!

The power of Walt's imagination was so dynamic, that he caused his world of animation to become a physical reality.

From within Walt's imagination, the first animated movie was brought into big screen movie reality. For it was here, that Walt's short feature film titled "Flowers and Trees", was introduced to the world!

Afterwards, came the reality of Walt's wonderful animated world, which he called, "Disney"! It is an understatement to say that Walt Disney's accomplishments were extraordinary!

These amazing animated possibilities that Walt's phenomenal imagination birthed into our world, now fills many hearts the world over, with strong inspiration!

Imagine-nations in pursuit of destined dreams!

If thou canst believe, all things are possible to him that believeth. **(Mark 9:23)**

Strong reason restores pursuit of destined purpose

It was a very strong reason that restored my desire, to continue pursuit towards fulfilling the purpose God destined for me.

It was a vision of seeing my children living out the designed dream they were destined for, within their lives.

A loving parent's ultimate desire is to see their children live a life of fulfilled purpose.

However at one time, I truly believed that my opportunity to ever witness this with my children, was totally destroyed.

This was because I abandoned my calling earlier in my christian walk, as a result of several missed ministry goal attempts and achievements.

The tragedy was that I lacked understanding concerning how influentially strong, walking in my own purpose was, towards inspiring my children to walk in theirs.

Therefore, my abandonment resulted in me failing to be that role model my three boys needed to see, while they were growing up.

However, through revelation about the heavenly vision, I was enlightened with clarity concerning the expected finish God desired for me to have. Which was a finish He already had planned out for my life.

You see dynamic, I discovered that God himself has a vision for the Kingdom, that he is destined to see manifested into the earth.

Look at what Paul reveals to us in the book of acts.

Where upon, O king Agrippa, I was not disobedient unto the heavenly vision: **(Acts 26:19)**

God's vision is to turn the picture of earth, into looking like a picture of heaven.

Look at what Jesus reveals to us in the book of Matthew, concerning the Fathers vision for the Kingdom.

Thy kingdom come, Thy will be done in earth, as it is in heaven. **(Matthew 6:10)**.

I discovered that God has a great future planned for me and my children, as we partnered with him to fulfill his vision of bringing heaven upon the earth.

Look at what the book of Jeremiah reveals to us.

For I know the plans and thoughts that I have for you,' says the Lord, plans for peace and well-being and not for disaster to give you a future and a hope. **(Jeremiah 29:11 Amp)**

God enlightened me to understand that his vision is to restore us back into his desired place for us, eden. That we may live a life of heaven upon the earth.

Look at what the book of Isaiah reveals to us.

For the Lord shall comfort Zion: he will comfort all her waste places; and he will make her wilderness like Eden, and her desert like the garden of the Lord; joy and gladness shall be found therein, thanksgiving, and the voice of melody. **(Isaiah 51:3)**

I discovered God's plan to use his own word in our mouth, that birth may be given to His heavenly vision.

Look at what the book of Isaiah reveals to us.

And I have put my words in thy mouth, and I have covered thee in the shadow of mine hand, that I may plant the heavens, and lay the foundations of the earth, and say unto Zion, Thou art my people. **(Isaiah 53:16)**

It was this profound enlightenment that empowered me to visualize my daughter walking in her purpose, while restoring confidence within me that my sons purpose's are destined as well.

As a result, I was reconnected back to God and began speaking life again, into visions and dreams upon the earth.

For believing to see my children one day walking in their destined purpose, was strong enough reason for me to bounce back and complete the assignment I was purposed for.

The Positive State motivational poster below,
(Motivational posters are tools of inspiration made available from the Positive State U platform, through social media, to promote personal development)
Attempts to inspire your pursuit towards discovery of purpose!

Positive State, Positive State U & Positive State University. Copyright 2016.
All rights reserved.

Finding Your Reason

You have been empowered with ability to
to overcome all the odds against you, and
experience destined success in life. This is due to
your royal relationship with God through Christ!

However, for you to experience success you were
destined for, it takes having a strong enough
reason for you to achieve your goal.

Visualize this possibility.
God desires to give you the world.

Look at what the book of Genesis reveals to us.

*Lift up now thine eyes, and look from the place
where thou art northward, and southward, and
eastward, and westward:*

*15 For all the land which thou seest, to thee will I
give it, and to thy seed for ever.*

(Genesis 13:14-15)

God desires for you to possess the promised land
and live a life of Eden success. His desire is the
strongest reason you can have, for taking action
to make destined success a manifested reality in
your life.

Hopefully, this book has inspired you to believe that with God, all things are possible.

As a child of God you were re-designed and re-positioned through Christ, back into your destined place of success! Therefore, no longer must you toil to achieve it! Just open your heart and receive it! Jesus has already accomplished your achievement of success, with his completed assignment at calvery. He declared your victory when a said, *"It is Finished!" (John 19:30).* therefore rejoice, if you have already accepted him as Lord and Savior, because you have accepted his finished works!

If you have not yet accepted him into your life, just ask him to come into your life and forgive you of your sins and he will, right now!

As a result of accepting his finished works, the Lord truly has made an inheritance available for you heavenly places in Christ for you!
(Ephesians 1:3).

Knowledge of this alone is strong reason enough, for you to pursue making it a reality in your life.

Here is the amazing part, God has already designed a purposed plan for you to follow, for you to obtain your promised land.
What can you imagine!

The Positive State motivational poster below,
(Motivational posters are tools of inspiration made available from the Positive State U platform, through social media, to promote personal development)
attempts to highlight Great Achievers who found reasons to accomplish phenomenal feats of Greatness!

Positive State, Positive State U & Positive State University. Copyright 2016. All rights reserved.

Understanding Your Destined Purpose!

Before you were born, there was a specific purpose for your life! God knew everything about you before you entered your mothers womb! What he had equipped you with! What gifts he would place in your life and the purpose those gifts were to accomplish!

Look at what the Lord revealed to Jeremiah!

*Before I formed thee in the belly I knew thee; and before thou came forth out of the womb I sanctified thee, and I ordained thee a prophet unto the nations **(Jeremiah 1:5)***

God designed you in his image, as a speaking spirit with the same capabilities to create and build up, as him!

*And God said, Let us make man in our image, after our likeness: **(Genesis 1:26)***
God designed you like him with these capabilities because he had a specific plan for you to fulfill within the earth!

*I know the plans and thoughts that I have for you,' says the Lord, 'plans for peace and well-being and not for disaster to give you a future and a hope. **(Jeremiah 29: 11 Amplified)***

God's plan from the beginning was to empower you with ability to rule over the earth, and complete his plan of planting the Eden picture of heaven upon the earth!

*And God blessed them, and God said unto them, Be fruitful, and multiply, and **replenish the earth,** and subdue it: and have dominion **(Genesis 1:28)**

Now that you have been restored through Christ back into your rightful place with our Father, The Lord's plan is to use your life to finish telling his story, along with advancing his Kingdom upon the earth!

As thou hast sent me into the world, even so have I also sent them into the world.

*Neither pray I for these alone, but for them also which shall believe on me through their word; **(John 17:18-20)***

He has replaced creative power back into your mouth with his wisdom, to bring whatever you can imagine in Him, into reality for the advancement of his Kingdom!

*For I will give you a mouth and wisdom, which all your adversaries shall not be able to gainsay nor resist. **(Luke 21:15)***

*And I have put my words in thy mouth, and I have covered thee in the shadow of mine hand, that I may plant the heavens, and lay the foundations of the earth, and say unto Zion, Thou art my people. **(Isaiah: 51:16)***

The Positive State motivational poster below,
(Motivational posters are tools of inspiration made available from the Positive State U platform, through social media, to promote personal development)
attempts to highlight he power of Understanding!

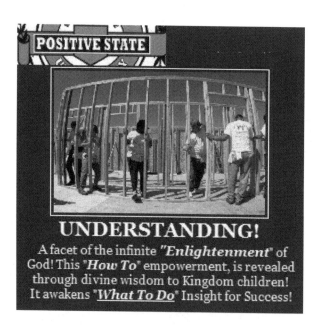

Positive State, Positive State U & Positive State University. Copyright 2016.
All rights reserved.

Give God something to work with!

Is there something that you love to do? What is that thing you like to do, that uplifts, encourages or inspires other people? That something, that you would find yourself doing, whether you were paid for doing it or not! Offer that gift to God for the advancement of His Kingdom! Begin there, and your gift will make room for you. Whatever you give God to work with, he will use and begin developing the message your life was designed to deliver!

Commit thy works unto the Lord, and thy thoughts shall be established. **(Proverbs 16:3)**

As you can see, you have been favored, empowered and setup to win! Becoming a total success in all areas of your life! This was Gods idea and intention for your life, before the foundation of the world.

Talking about the power of a strong enough reason?

Take a glimpse at Jesus! His reason for fulfilling his Fathers desire was to have you restored back into your rightful place with him! The picture of seeing you returned back unto the father, produced great joy within the heart of Jesus!

So much joy, that it strengthened his confidence to the point where he could endure taking on the price of the cross!

Take a look at what the book of Hebrews says,

Looking unto Jesus the author and finisher of our faith; who for the joy that was set before him endured the cross, despising the shame, and is set down at the right hand of the throne of God. (Hebrews 12:2)

The Lords reason to see you restored back into your right standing with the father, was strong enough for Jesus to allow soldiers to thrust thorns through his head, until it gushed out his blood.
Restoring you back to the place of being one hundred percent whole in ever area of your life, was the assignment of Jesus!

The works that he finished upon calvary provided a strong enough reason for you, to no longer accept defeat from your enemy within any area of your life.

Concerning your total healing, Jesus took thirty nine blood gushing lashes on his back, to destroy sickness and disease within your life!

Concerning your total provision, Jesus allowed men to drive thick nails straight through his hand, to destroy the curse of poverty, lack and insufficiency forever in your life.

Concerning your Freedom, Jesus allowed those same men to drive nails into his feet, that you may walk upon the earth in dominating authority! Totally free from bondage within your life!

This is how powerful a strong enough reason is!

It is powerful enough to inspire the almighty God to come off his throne, put limitations on his unlimited power, then humble himself unto death, though he is total life himself! Just so that you could be repositioned back into your winning space of success in life.

The fathers only desire now is to reveal unto you all of his secrets from the Kingdom, that you and your family may experience living a life of heavenly paradise in Eden upon the earth. While fulfilling your destined purpose of being a blessing to others, that all the families of the earth may be blessed!

Look at what the book of Deuteronomy reveals to us!

The secret things belong unto the Lord our God: but those things which are revealed belong unto us and to our children for ever, that we may do all the words of this law. **(Deuteronomy 29:29)**

The power of a strong enough reason!

The End

Positive State, Positive State U & Positive State University. Copyright 2016.
All rights reserved

Conclusion

Thanks Phenomenal, for making the time to discover the powerful message within this E-book.
It's purpose was to simply to borrow your imagination and give you a glimpse of the " *Dynamic* " wealth that's hidden within you, along with the purposeful force that a strong enough reason can have on a God, just to see your inner wealth unlocked. You are phenomenal and possess treasures of inner greatness that is very much needed within the earth.
Go forth and release your inner greatness, you're phenomenal!

The Positive State motivational poster below,
(Motivational posters are tools of inspiration made available from the Positive State U platform, through social media, to promote personal development)
attempts to highlight how phenomenal your inner treasures of greatness truly are.

Positive State, Positive State U & Positive State University. Copyright 2016. All rights reserved.

A Empowering Video Training Series

Positive State, Positive State U & Positive State University. Copyright 2016. All rights reserved.

Download Your Copy Today!

Visit us at:

http://www.positivestateu.com/

follow us
on
Facebook & Instagram!

Made in the USA
San Bernardino, CA
03 May 2017